DESIGN
and decorate
BEDROOMS

NEW HOLLAND

Lesley Taylor

With thanks to Mum and Dad for all their encouragement and support, and to Coral, Yvonne and Emma from New Holland for helping me to transform my knowledge into a beautiful collection of books.

First published in 1998 by
New Holland (Publishers) Ltd
London • Cape Town • Sydney • Singapore

24 Nutford Place
London W1H 6DQ
United Kingdom

80 McKenzie Street
Cape Town 8001
South Africa

3/2 Aquatic Drive
Frenchs Forest, NSW 2086
Australia

ISBN 1 85368 932 7 (hbk)
ISBN 1 85368 933 5 (pbk)

Managing Editor: Coral Walker
Special photography: Janine Hosegood
Designed by: Grahame Dudley Associates
Editor: Emma Callery

Reproduction by Modern Age Repro House Ltd, Hong Kong
Printed and bound in Singapore by Tien Wah Press (Pte) Ltd

Contents

Introduction

There are no hard and fast rules when decorating a bedroom. This means that time must be taken to ensure the deceptions you make are the best for you and fulfil your individual brief for colour style, storage requirements and the finishing touches.

This book has been specially designed to inform you of all the options available for good bedroom design, so that you feel confident enough to make a decision that is an informed one. This means that you will then achieve the room of your dreams without costly and time-consuming mistakes.

The book will guide you through the planning stages, help you make decisions on lighting and storage and assist you in making the all-important choices regarding the best style and colour scheme for your room.

Questions such as, 'what elements will help me to create a cottage bedroom?', 'How do I ensure my child's bedroom will be an area that can be adapted as his or her needs change?' or, 'How do I create a half tester?', are all answered in simple terms. There is also a section on bed linen and soft furnishings. So, all in all, *Design and Decorate Bedrooms* contains everything that you need to create a beautiful and practical bedroom for you, your family and your friends.

Happy designing.

Planning the
perfect bedroom

Planning the layout for your bedroom is an important part of the design process as it ensures, for example, that you have chosen the best position for the bed and have ample room for your chosen style of storage or furniture. By considering all your options, you may discover ways to free up space so that you could include a seating area, say, or you may discover that you have ample floor space to erect a partition, creating a walk-in dressing room or even an en suite bath or shower room. You will be surprised at how different a room appears when you view it as a flat floor plan.

To make a floor plan, simply draw out your room to scale on graph paper. Use every square centimetre (or inch) on the graph to represent a unit of distance in your room. For example, 1:20 scale means that 1 cm (1 in) on your scaled drawing represents 20 cm (20 in) in your room, and so on. Measure your room using an extending metal tape, and make sure that you include electrical points and windows on your plan. Skirting, architraves and dado rails should also be considered as they can obstruct pieces of furniture.

Once you have drawn the outline of the room, draw and cut out templates of the various items to be included such as the bed, wardrobes and chairs. Use the same scale as the floor plan.

MAKING THE MOST OF IT
▼ Drawing an elevation will help you determine the best height for furniture allowing access to features like windows.

If you have sloping ceilings or any unusual features that can restrict the head room, or furniture height, then these areas should be drawn as an elevation on a separate piece of paper. This will help you to determine whether the items will fit comfortably into the space available. To use your elevation, you will need to draw and cut out the pieces of furniture, again to scale, but this time showing their height and width, as opposed to the length and depth, as required for a floor plan.

Once this is complete you can move the pieces of furniture around the plan, and try them on the elevation until you

PARTITIONED OFF

▲ A simple timber partition can release floor space within a large bedroom to be used as a dressing room or en suite bathroom. Ensure you continue any architectural detailing on the partition, to make it look original.

achieve the best layout for your room. Don't forget to allow for doors and those on wardrobes opening into the room, and the distance that drawers pull out. Ample floor space should also be allocated around the bed.

Once a suitable plan has been decided, draw the items onto the floor plan and elevation. I find it is then best to leave these plans for a day or two before starting work; you can then take a fresh look to see that no mistakes have been made. Now is also a good time to check that there are sufficient electrical sockets for your requirements and that light fittings are in the relevant positions for your chosen layout (see pages 76-7 for additional information on lighting).

HIDDEN SPACE
▲ Traditional rooms with fireplaces often have alcoves on each side – the ideal position for fitted wardrobes.

The bed is most probably the largest item of furniture to be included in the space, and should be placed where it allows maximum movement around the room. It need not be central to the room, as positioning it off-centre can quite often make more floor space available, but beware of placing a double bed in the corner of a room as this restricts the access to one side. This position can be successful with single beds, however.

If you have the space, create a dressing room with a timber and plasterboard partition or put a large open shelving unit 1 m (1 yd) from the back wall. Place the bed in front of it and access to your dressing area can be gained from either side.

CAREFUL PLANNING

▼ A shelf positioned between two sets of wardrobes offers alternative storage behind the bed if there is no room for bedside cabinets.

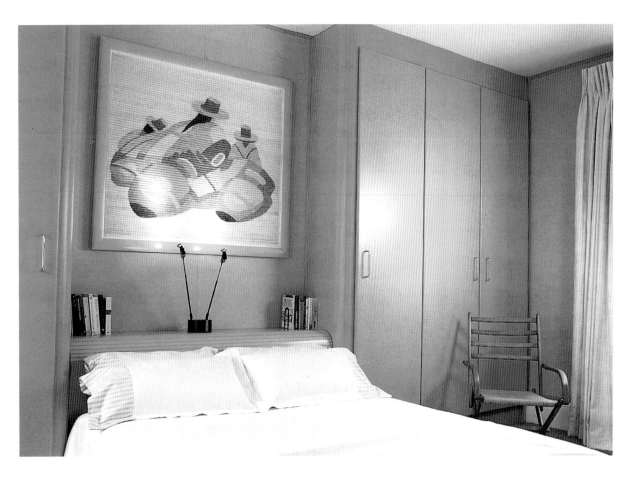

STYLE *file*

The style in which you decide to decorate your bedroom must be a personal one; and as the room is normally only seen by close friends and family, it does not have to follow the main theme of the rest of the house. Of course, while practicalities such as ample storage and a comfortable layout are important and should be given due consideration, the most important thing about designing a bedroom is that you feel totally relaxed and comfortable in your own private space. After all, it is a sanctuary and retreat – a room in which to pamper yourself and forget all the worries of the outside world.

Certain styles appeal more to one individual than another. For example, you may prefer a truly opulent air, with heavy brocade or damask bed drapes, and even a chandelier or two. And why not? Of, if your have the pleasure of working in such salubrious surroundings all day, then you may wish to come home and relax in a simple bedroom containing nothing more than concealed storage and a very comfortable bed in which to forget the rich trappings of your daily routine. Whatever you decide upon, the array of soft furnishings and decorative accessories now available is outstanding, and you will have no problem purchasing items to suit your preferences.

TOP LEFT
Many people find they
feel most relaxed in a
totally coordinated
bedroom, but it can be
too overpowering. Here,
only the soft furnishings
are coordinated.

BOTTOM LEFT
Balance plays an all
important part here, with
the bed placed centrally
in the room and the
accessories are carefully
positioned on either side.

TOP RIGHT
A glorious retreat for
the owner of this
house. Rich terracotta
and gold add a richness
and opulence to a room
full of Oriental and
Eastern accessories.

BOTTOM RIGHT
If you have a busy daily
schedule, or work within
a visual environment, this
truly minimal bedroom is
the perfect place in which
to unwind or to focus your
creative thoughts.

Contemporary style

SHARP DESIGN
▼ Modern lines are clean and hard-edged. A graphic bedstead in gun metal steel forms the nucleus of the bedroom decor. Keep colours bold and striking or neutral and under-stated. Select a stylized standard lamp for an unusual bedside light.

The word contemporary means of the same age or era. In design terms, therefore, it means that the contemporary interior is something that is current, and of this period, and as there are currently so many design trends upon which to draw, it gives a very broad spectrum indeed for planning a bedroom.

Two of the most obvious styles for a contemporary bedroom that most readily spring to mind are rooms furnished in a minimalist manner, and those decorated with neutral colours and natural furnishings. Shades of beige and cream accompanied by seagrass matting with textured cottons and linens sit very comfortably together. Either way, the room will have a distinctly contemporary feel to it.

One of the most pleasing things about this type of styling is that it does not have to follow an historical or period style. The purist approach to decor need not be pursued and if you have furniture from a mixture of eras and in a range of styles, there is every possibility that you can find a suitable way of uniting them. The other element that is becoming increasingly used in the contemporary interior is the influence of other cultures. Adopt the ideas wholesale or adapt them to fit in with your environment. In all, contemporary style gives enormous freedom and can afford you the opportunity of being very creative.

CONTRASTING COLOURS

▲ Modern colours and check fabrics give this room its contemporary feel. Combining green and blue might not immediately strike you as being a great idea. However, as you can see, they work together surprisingly well. Tester pots of paint are invaluable for experimenting.

NEUTRALITY

◀ Natural or neutral colour schemes consist of a blend of creams through to brown, plus the non-colours white and black. A successful room will have a variety of textures and tones, adding interest and depth to the room.

Shaker simplicity
provides harmony

The name Shaker derives from an American sect founded in 1747. Their individual approach to design produced a truly functional range of furniture and furnishings which lacked ornamentation and decoration. This style has once again become popular, and simple, well-designed and practical rooms can be created in this truly contemporary style.

All the elements in a Shaker bedroom are functional, so your eye is drawn to shape and proportion rather than colour or decorative detail. Despite this emphasis on function and simplicity, a Shaker room lacks nothing in a design sense.

SOFTLY SIMPLE
▼ Shaker interiors can be nothing but simple. The belief in purity and simplicity extended from the Shakers' form of worship into the styling of their homes and furnishings.

Plain walls are an integral part of this style of decor, with natural fabrics and both painted and natural wood playing a very important part. Any well-made piece of furniture with graceful lines works well in this setting, as do fabrics such as muslin, gingham, linen and cotton. If you feel the need for pattern, use simple checks and stripes and keep floral prints to a minimum. Opt, too, for muted shades.

The colours used here are soft and there is nothing jarring in the scheme, so the room has a tranquil atmosphere. The colours of both walls and floor appear in the soft furnishings, giving a harmony to the space. The shutters give the room privacy, but simple off-white blinds or curtains would have been a successful alternative if you were looking for something a little softer. Note the detailing on the curtain at the head of the bed. The tabbed heading creates soft folds in the fabric without a fussy gathered effect, and although it is quite plain, it is an effective piece of detailing in the room.

Fresh flowers in an earthenware jug add just a splash of colour, together with the other simple accessories on either side of the bed: the vine and lavender wreath bound with a short length of gingham ribbon and the terracotta jug standing on the chest of drawers. Finally, no Shaker look would be complete without the most well-known of Shaker items – the oval timber boxes. Here they are stacked neatly on the table by the window.

SIMPLE STORAGE

◀ This traditional Shaker box is larger than the standard storage boxes and is designed specifically for laundry.

SAME SHADES, DIFFERENT PATTERNS

▼ When choosing fabrics, look for designs that feature the same colours used in different ways. This can add variety within unity.

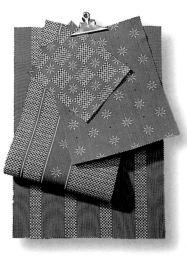

Sleek new art meets
tribal culture

HAND CARVED
▲ Traditional wood-carvings make beautiful additions to any room, especially in a bedroom with a tribal theme.

Tribal design has been popular for quite a time, illustrating as it does the rich history, cultures and philosophies of many different ethnic groups. The room shown opposite, for example, has a rustic charm, with a simple beamed ceiling and a ceramic floor which works particularly well with the chosen fabrics. In fact, the room and its elements look as if they truly belong together. The colours used in the tribal designs originate from natural dyes and colour pigments and it is the continuity of these colours into the main colour scheme that is the secret to the room's decorative success.

As the bedding makes such a design statement, pattern elsewhere in the room has been kept to a minimum, with accessories providing the detail. Especially noticeable, of course, are the paintings which have been chosen for their appropriate colours rather than subject matter. The one exception is the tribal mask, currently residing on the bed, which serves to remind us of the starting point for this decorative theme. The positioning of the rich wooden furniture adds balance to the room. If, for example, the far wall did not have the mahogany chest of drawers, the foreground would outweigh the rear of the room, making it appear off balance.

SETTING THE SCENE
▶ The addition of one item of furniture or fabric can have a profound effect on a room. This oriental chest, for example, would certainly set the tone of a bedroom. Imagine how different the bedroom featured opposite would appear if the bedding were replaced with a different style of cover.

It is interesting to note that the main bedding is made up

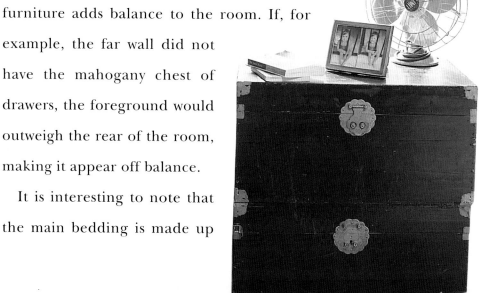

NEW ART

▲ Modern anglepoise lamps and metal sculptures team perfectly with traditional patterns and designs of Africa and Australasia. An electic mix – the style works well because the lines, images and colours are vivid and bold.

of black, cream, brown and mustard. Although this combination adds depth to the room, it does not contribute to the warmth that the scheme obviously has. Instead, the designer has cleverly introduced warm red tones into the room via a cushion in the centre of the bed (it also contains the other, earthy, bed cover colours), and an abstract painting hanging above it. When these combine with the naturally mellow tones of the mahogany furniture scattered around the bedroom, they add the warmth the colour scheme needs.

Refreshingly modern feel
with traditional

You may find when decorating your home that there are elements from many different decorative styles that appeal to you. You may like traditional fabrics and wallcoverings but dislike frills and fussy interiors, or you may like clean lines and simplicity, but not favour the harsh, clinical feel of many contemporary settings. If this is the case, find a way of successfully combining the elements from each style to create a contemporary decor of your very own. This is precisely what the owner of this bedroom has achieved. The room has a classical appearance, but as there are no fussy soft furnishings, it has clean lines and simplicity.

The wallcovering features a traditional oriental pattern. There are many archive fabrics and wallcoverings in this style so they are readily available from interior design outlets. The flooring, too, is an eastern design of a floral pattern set within a larger geometric border. Finally, the scatter cushion on the bed is made from a rose print fabric which, although not oriental in its design, picks up on the floral wallpaper and tones in so well with the colour scheme.

When you consider the approach taken by the decorator, it is, in fact, the opposite of what is frequently done at home. Many people choose relatively plain walls and floors and opt for the bed as a central feature, quite often covering it in the most vibrant pattern in the room. This alternative approach is very refreshing. Here the bed nestles into the colour scheme, rather than dominating what is, after all, a relatively small room.

CHINOISERIE
▼ There has long been an interest in Chinese-style textiles and wallcoverings, and many copies of archive designs are now reproduced, giving access to this traditional style of wallcovering.

elements

Accessories have been equally well chosen in this room. The standard trees on each side of the bed work well with the simple, sheer curtains framing them. The symmetry, initially suggested by the windows and furthered by the trees, is enhanced by the positioning of the two bedside tables. They may not be the same shape or height, but this just adds to the originality of this contemporary-styled bedroom.

MIXING AND MATCHING
▲ This room has a mixture of traditional furnishings. Yet because of the striking panel behind the bed, the overall look is one of oriental tranquility.

Traditional style

CLASSICAL SCHEME
▼ Very traditional elements are brought together. Note the iron and brass bedstead and reading lamp, the wooden bedside cabinet – the bed linen, too is classic: lace-edged cotton, hand-embroidered sheets and a deep-dyed, glazed coverlet in crimson and forest green.

Many people find they feel most comfortable in a traditionally designed room. There is always a sense of familiarity rooted in the past, and the scope for achieving an attractive, comfortable bedroom where you can relax and unwind is wonderfully wide. Traditional rooms can either be decorated in a purist style, taking one historical period and sticking to it, or by mixing various themes you can create an individual, yet nevertheless traditional, room. Romantic, frilly and feminine, homespun simplicity, or rich and masculine are all decorative approaches which sit quite happily beneath the traditional umbrella. With such versatility at your fingertips, you can create a number of different looking bedrooms in the one traditionally decorated home.

In the 1980s, traditional styling was relaunched as an interior design trend, and the simpler approach was replaced by ornate, floral, chintz curtaining, brass bedsteads and patchwork throws. Other traditional styles include elaborate Empire bedheads and swags and tails at the windows in that sumptuous nineteenth-century European style, or antique linen and lace to create a softer, prettier bedroom. Look through magazines and books to decide which style appeals the most; then combine patterns and colours accordingly.

TRADITIONAL COORDINATION

▶ Soft furnishings have a great impact on the finished look of a room, and now many archive fabrics and wallcoverings are being manufactured, enabling the home designer to achieve an authentic look quickly and easily.

TRADITIONAL PROPORTIONS

▼ High ceilings, floor-length windows and feature fireplace are the perfect backdrop for a grand scheme. However, the simpler, yet equally elegant, approach taken in this bedroom has resulted in a very warm and restful area.

Stylish classics
in gold

Colour can have such a pronounced effect on your mood that careful consideration should always be taken when choosing it for your home. Nowhere is this more important than in the bedroom which, for most people, is a sanctuary from everyday life.

This room has used a combination of clever decorating tricks: the warm gold used here is one of the most comforting in the spectrum; the stripes in the wallpaper add height to the room, while the plain cream curtains and bed drapes with their beautifully scrunched headings add softness. (To achieve this, make the curtains very full – at least three times the width of the space – and sew very deep casings. Stuff the casings with spare fabric for a puffy effect.)

The fabric is a clever device as stripes can often add a harsh formality to a room. Patterned glazed cotton introduced on the headboard and scatter cushions draw attention to the bed and bring together all the main colours in the room.

The bed has been dressed in white bed linen; many people would not consider using white in a scheme with so much cream, but it actually adds a crispness, and white used directly next to cream always makes for a richer look. A deep green has been selected for the bed valance, and this colour is echoed on the headboard.

Lighting is very important in a bedroom, not only for practical use but it can highlight areas, such as a dressing table,

TRICK OF THE LIGHT
◄ Select an ornate style of lamp for a bedroom such as this to follow through the classical theme.

and cream

adding a further dimension to the scheme.

Finally, attention to detail is important here: the classic bed-side lamps, the picture hung from oversized tassels over the bed, and the fabric rose on the tieback all provide visual interest.

CLEVER HEADINGS

◀ A puffed curtain heading above the bed and as a matching window treatment is easy to create yet provides a chic and eye-catching finish.

Gilt and white linen
create French-style

'Less is more' has always been my approach to home decorating, and here a careful blend of antique furniture and simple furnishings is the perfect example of such a philosophy. Keeping things simple does not mean that the end result need be bland or uninteresting. If fact, a well-chosen object carefully positioned can have more of an impact on a room than a collection of more elaborate items.

The warm, yet neutral, shades used on the walls and floor create the perfect backdrop to the rich antique coffer and linen press. The gilded cane bedhead adds a French air to the room and works particularly well in a room of this proportion (a dark mahogany headboard would have made it look heavier and more crowded).

Simple cream curtaining softens the hard edges of the sash windows while also adding to the lightness of the colour scheme. Note how the crisp white bed linen and cream curtaining give the light walls a richer colour. This is a good trick to remember as, in rooms with little sunlight or those that are on the small side, it is good to be able to achieve a richness but without making the room heavy and dark.

While the majority of this colour scheme is in neutral tones, a cream and

SOFT CONTRASTS

▼ When considering a colour scheme, the upholstery on a chair is as important as the chair itself, as both need to fit comfortably into the finished room. If you upholster a chair in a fabric that is tonally similar to the finish on the wood, as here, the addition of a contrasting cushion will normally add life and depth to its appearance. But, as you can see, it does not necessarily have to be a striking contrast.

elegance

opaline toile de Jouy fabric has been selectively used as a bed valance, a practical Roman blind and to upholster the two Regency, brass-mounted chairs at the foot of the bed. This fabric adds delicate detail without detracting from the room's uncluttered appearance.

As with all well-decorated rooms, accessories play an important part. The floor-length gilt mirror in the far corner of the room opens out what could have been a dull, dark space. The plants and flowers add life and additional colour, and they tie in beautifully with the botanical prints above the bed.

NEUTRALITY

▲ Creams, buttermilks and whites work beautifully together. However, to create a successful scheme you need contrast of tone – here provided by the dark wooden furniture – to add punctuation to the room. Imagine this room with pale wooden or painted furniture – the overall effect would lack depth and richness.

The timeless appeal of
lustrous wood

PLAIDS AND CHECKS

▼ Rich colours are perfect for a traditional colour scheme, and if you choose to combine reproduction furniture with modern furnishings, traditional accessories will ensure the end result is authentic.

Reproduction furniture and modern furnishings have been used to create this very traditional, truly masculine, and richly coloured bedroom. The proportions of the room are responsible for the bedroom's formal quality, which is far more reminiscent of the grander town and country houses of the past than the new properties built today.

While the room is large, it is nevertheless comfortable and

and rich tartan

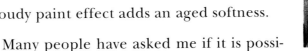

PLAID PATTERN
▶ Tartans and plaids always evoke a sense of history. Once only available in wool, these traditional patterns are now found in shiny, satinized cottons, silks, and manmade fabrics, as well as wall and floor-coverings.

welcoming due to its chosen colour scheme. The colourwashed terracotta walls help to draw in the room, making it more comfortable, and although terracotta can be a strong and dominating colour, the cloudy paint effect adds an aged softness.

Many people have asked me if it is possible to mix checks and plaids successfully; I think this room gives you the answer – as long as you follow a few simple rules. First, the colours must work successfully within your chosen colour scheme and, second, be aware of proportion. As with mixing any patterns, choose designs with varying size and intensity of motif; fabrics with a solid background work well with those that have a lighter, open background. For example, small busy checks benefit from being teamed with larger check designs that echo one or two of the colours in the smaller check fabric. It is not just the proportion of the patterns that count, however. One design should dominate, and any additional designs should be used in lesser quantities. In this way, no two patterns compete.

The main quantity of plaid in this room is used for the curtains and pillow covers. In addition, three designs are introduced as throws and blankets, each of which has a different background colour, giving an individual intensity of tone and design. Not one of the designs threatens the main fabric, and the amount of plain green fabric used on the bed and chairs prevents the plaids and checks from making the room too fussy.

Tranquil bedrooms

Calm, pleasant, at ease, and serene, are all terms that describe the tranquil room. With this in mind, the best way to create such a haven in one's home is by avoiding busy patterns and bright colours. Instead, go for the cooler, more relaxing colours of the spectrum such as greens, aquamarines and neutral creams. Pattern can be used successfully within these schemes, but choose soft, flowing or smudgy designs in muted shades rather than bold or definite patterns: understatement is the key to success when seeking to style a peaceful bedroom.

The tranquil room can be a challenge to the home decorator as the aim of the finished scheme must be a place that is comfortable and sedate, yet full of detail and interest. In a period setting, layer textured fabrics like lace and patchwork in the colours mentioned above. Remember, too, that softly painted timber and canework will add individual texture but without detracting from the overall atmosphere.

A more contemporary setting will benefit from simple detailing on the curtain heads, say, or consider plain Roman blinds with a hint of colour added by contrast borders. Or make a throw or two for the bed from textured fabrics, like loosely woven woollens, natural linens and slubby cottons. These fabrics add interest and retain the overall peace of the bedroom.

NATURAL TEXTILES

▼ Recently, natural textiles have become very popular and they are most successfully used when textures and patterns are mixed to create an interesting, yet restrained, interior.

TRADITIONAL TRANQUILITY

▼ In this attic bedroom, pretty print wallpapers and borders have been replaced by textured layers of cream, white and soft peach to create a peaceful haven.

SHADES OF CREAM

◀ The colour wheel is extremely powerful, and harnessing its powers is the key to a successul interior. The cool colours from the left-hand side of the wheel create a calm, spacious setting.

Cream, oyster and ivory
create calm

Throughout this book you will see some wonderful examples of neutral colour schemes. Part of the joy of using these colours is that because they are so versatile, they look equally at home in a traditional or a contemporary setting. So, to set the theme, make use of the furniture and accessories.

The beautiful room featured opposite has both traditional and contemporary elements that combine to create a very individual and restful environment. The stylish wrought iron bed and occasional pieces of furniture are suitably traditional and they contrast nicely with the refreshing approach to soft furnishings that has been adopted. While bed canopies and curtain pelmets are all a part of the traditional school of decorating, not a frill or a swag is on display here. Instead, a mixture of patterned and plain fabrics, add detail.

A practical quilt cover and valance (easy to remove, and easy to wash) have been chosen to dress the bed, and with the addition of throws in various tones and designs and crisp simple cushions, the effect is restful yet sumptuous.

The room is not particularly large, yet it has a very high and shapely ceiling. Note the tricks the designer has used to reduce the appearance of its height. The window, for example, is tall and narrow but because the curtains are the same colour and tone as the walls this is not exaggerated

DECORATIVE DETAILING
▲ Mixing natural coloured fabrics gives you the opportunity to make the most of design details. The satin edging and pompoms used on these wonderful cushions add interest but take nothing away from the overall harmonious look.

SOFTENED HUES
◄ Aged or distressed pieces of wooden furniture have a softness to them which work particularly well in a tranquil interior.

and comfort

as it would be with curtains of a deeper colour or tone. Furthermore, with the addition of a Roman blind, the window height is subtly reduced, giving the whole wall a better proportion. The carefully positioned pictures also help to draw down the eye line, as does the bed drape: its generous band of fabric hangs towards the front of the bed.

KEEPING IT SIMPLE
▼ In a relatively small bedroom, choose your occasional furniture carefully. It should be practical and offer additional storage, but without overpowering the room.

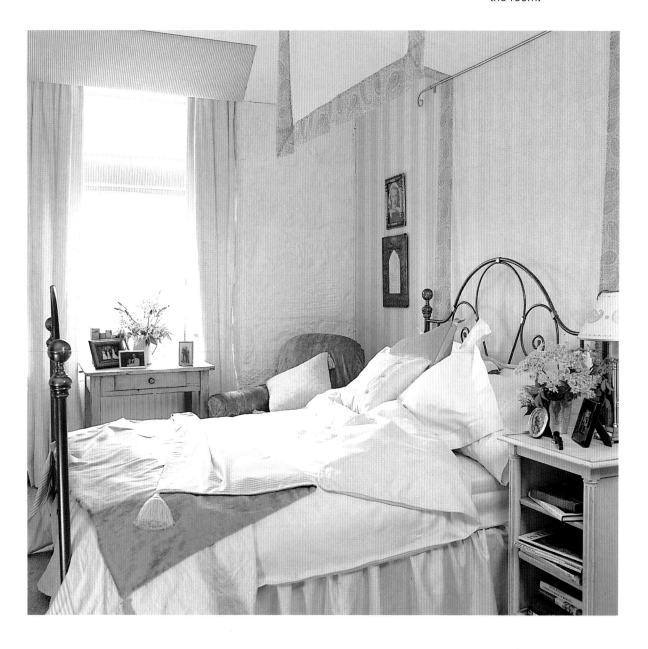

Restful retreat uses
shades of

Stylish and practical is the way this room is best described. Almost every element has been chosen for its form and function, and all you could possibly need in the bedroom is catered for here. First and foremost, there is the simple bed that lacks the fussiness of a headboard or bed drapes. Then there is the storage – a wardrobe with its green stained wooden doors – and, finally, a blanket chest positioned beneath a single shelf, which in itself offers an additional storage and display area. This restful, uncluttered room must surely make for peaceful living.

cool green

The floor covering is equally practical. The hard wooden floor has been successfully softened with a large rug to add some warmth underfoot. The natural materials bring life to the room and the neutral tones blend most harmoniously with the *eau-de-Nil* walls. The wooden shutters create a wonderful filtered light and offer privacy without the addition of colour or pattern that curtains would provide. However, notice how a hint of softness, in the form of softly draped muslin, has been added above the shutters. This touch of romance just breaks up the hard lines that might otherwise detract from the overall atmosphere of this room.

Finishing touches like a large mirror, a comfortable chair, and a small display table, complete the list of practical 'must haves' for a plain bedroom. However, uncluttered living need not necessarily mean bare living, and the soft furnishings comfortably redress the balance. The piped cushions on the chair make it most welcoming and the ties at the top of the back cushion are attractive – and, of course, practical – decorative details. Without them, the cushions would be far too liable to slip around. Likewise, the lace-trimmed pillows add a little luxury to the bedding. The lightweight cotton throw and zigzag, lacy edging on the bed valance tone in beautifully with the walls and this pale, pale shade of green maintains the bedroom's light and airy, and above all, calm ambience.

PAINT IT
▲ Simple pale green and off-white paints can add serenity to a room in a way that few other colours can achieve.

Clean lines -
h a r m o n i o u s   t o n e s

A minimalist approach to decorating has been adopted in this clean-cut and peaceful room. You should be careful when choosing this type of scheme as lines can sometimes appear hard and clinical. However, the use of a soft colourwashed paint effect, as here, disguises the harsh linear effect that plain painted walls could have produced. As a result, the sharp lines of the granite topped table and the geometric artwork are softened. Rather than a room of hard corners – which would be far from tranquil – there is a sense of serenity.

The room also has a warmth and softness to it not always associated with the more minimalist of colour schemes. The reason for this is the blend of wall colour and the mellow, natural wooden floorboards. A warm, mellow colour scheme always offers a welcoming atmosphere. Colourwashing is very simple to achieve: after the first coat of emulsion paint has been applied and left to dry, use a wide paintbrush and a second shade of paint diluted with water 5:1. Apply the paint quickly and over small areas at a time, swirling the brush in different directions to achieve a soft effect. Leave to dry and repeat with another colour, diluted in the same way.

To live successfully in such a sparse room you should strive to be neat and tidy, as even the smallest

FAUX EFFECTS
◀ If you are unable to afford real marble – some excellent fake effect finishes are available at considerably less cost.

LIGHT STYLE
◀ Lighting is a key to a mellow bedroom. Free-standing or side table lamps can provide style as well as a congenial ambience.

misplaced item could ruin the order of the scheme. In addition,
spend time choosing the correct type of storage; it should completely satisfy your needs yet be in keeping with the minimal
theme of the room: aim for functional, but unobtrusive.

Lighting is also very important for a simple decorative scheme
like this one. To be successful, it should add peaks and troughs
of light, giving tonal variety to the room. The variation in wall
colouring between the bedroom and en suite bathroom is created by different forms of lighting, giving an extra dimension to
the finished rooms.

**KEEPING IT
SIMPLE**
▲ Simple lines and
mellow colours from the
warm side of the colour
wheel offer a very
stylish solution to those
who like a bedroom that
is uncluttered and
ordered.

Opulent style

At one time, this style of decoration would only have been seen in the larger country and town houses in which it originated. However, as the barriers of formal interior design have been slowly replaced by a more 'personal preference' approach to decorating, this is no longer the hard-and-fast rule. Coronas and half testers are now commonplace, and damasks, silks and brocades have become part of a designer's stock-in-trade.

Bear all this in mind, because the bedroom is the one room in the home where you can feel free to choose a style that may not be in keeping with the rest of your home. It is normally your own private space, an area viewed by only a few close family or friends, and so practical decoration need not be a priority.

The key to opulent style is the use of rich textures and colours, of heavily dressed windows and beds, with an abundance of detailing like fringing, lace, braiding and passementerie of all kinds. An opulent room does not have to appear fussy and frilly, however. Rather, it should endeavour to provide an air of grandeur and elegance. Antique pieces of furniture always look at home in this setting, an ornate mahogany bedhead, for example, may be the perfect starting point if choosing this style of decor for a bedroom.

DEEP SHADES

◀ Start with a beautiful carved headboard, such as the delightful French one shown here. Add rich silks and damasks, heavy brocades and velvets. Then trim with lace-covered bolsters, plump cushions, tassels, braiding and ostentatious passementerie. Choose deep jewel colours: burgundy, old gold, sapphire blue, forest green and ruby.

GOLD AND CREAM

▲ The ceiling height is perfect for this type of decorative treatment. The corona and bed drapes have plenty of design detail, but the simplicity of the window treatment and the clean lines redress the room's balance. These elements have been combined to create luxury without fuss.

SILK AND LACE

◀ Even if the remainder of the room has a minimal amount of soft furnishings, the bed is always the one place you can dress lavishly. Crisp cotton with satin and lace is timeless and great piles of pillows add to the sense of opulence.

Scarlet stripe
for regal splendour

This red and cream room is decorated in typical Regency style. The walls have been panelled both above and below the dado with a relief moulding which has been highlighted in cream. Note how the wall has been split by the dado about a third of the way up the wall. This gives traditional proportions to the room, rather than the more Mediterranean effect of a dado placed approximately 30 cm (12 in) higher.

The wall outside the panels has been painted in scarlet, the main colour of the room, and a dark red glaze has been used on a cream base within the panelling to create a woodgrain paint effect. This is quite soft but also gives a striped effect. Many people would have been tempted to use a formal striped wallcovering within the panels when trying to create a classical Regency-style room. But imagine the room if this style of paper had been used. It would have been totally overpowering, and very hard on the eye. Instead, by using a 'dragging' technique with paint, the overall look is gentler.

The arched windows are a very clever design detail which further soften the room with their ruched drapes. As you look through the curtains you can just detect the almost square pains of glass in the French doors which have been disguised by sheer curtains. If there were no sheers, the door design may have detracted from the arches, themselves a much needed relief from all the square angles of this panelled room.

ROSE RED

◀ Isn't it interesting to see how the same basic colour scheme can look when it is given a different design style? Here the addition of a soft country floral bedspread and casual bed drapes offer a far more contemporary finish to a bedroom.

The bedstead has also been chosen for its soft and flowing design, yet another contrast to the walls. The bed area holds some other very important design details, too. A pair of gilt night tables positioned on each side of the bed add a much needed colour contrast and the frilled bed cushions and the buttoned damask bedspread add a slightly feminine touch to an otherwise masculine room.

AFFLUENT SPLENDOUR

◀ Panelled walls, Regency stripes and damask fabrics all originated in the days of opulent styling, and they still create the same affluent atmosphere.

Ruches, gathers
and frills provide

FANTASY FABRICS

▼ Yellow and blue is currently thought of as a modern combination of colours. However, this traditional and gregarious room shows it has long been appreciated.

Here is possibly the ultimate in fantasy furnishings. The gathered and frilled canopy above the bed has been lined with gold, picking up one of the colours from the principal striped fabric. Then the balloon draping that spills so extravagantly to the floor has been pulled back to look almost Moorish in its influence and featuring plenty of ornate tassels. Notice how the bedhead has been upholstered in a style that reflects the ruching on

a stately setting

SHEER DELIGHT
▲ For an opulent setting, choose silks, damasks and brocades to accompany gilt accessories such as clocks, mirrors and picture frames.

the canopy, and how the gold bedspread also matches the canopy's lining above. Yet while it is full of detail, the finished effect is not as claustrophobic as that of many other four poster designs, because its proportions are so generous.

The silk fabric used on the bed ties in beautifully with other colours in the room. The colour scheme is primarily gold and blue, but the salmon pink in the stripe acts as the perfect contrast. It lifts the scheme and gives the opportunity to introduce items into the room like the side lamp with its pink shade.

The beautiful wooden floor has been partly covered with a traditional rug in a yellow and blue geometric design. This is a happy complement to the soft stripe of the silk fabric, and its light tones open up the floor area, creating spaciousness while providing comfort.

Carefully selected pieces of furniture and accessories are an all-important ingredient in this style of decor. Genuine or faux antique pieces are placed strategically to provide a sense of history and establishment. The gilded mirror, for example, is generous in its detailing, and opulent in its style. The Regency chairs, upholstered in a yellow and black animal print, are a novel and exotic touch. It would be all too easy for a bedroom like this to look like a museum piece and not lived in. However, the family photographs and books next to the bed are reassuring in their normality.

Country & cottage

If the mellow tones of antique pine appeal to you, and patchwork quilts and home-spun accessories are high on your list of decorative priorities, then country or cottage styling is for you.

There is always a welcoming softness to this style of decor. Formal is a word that cannot be found in the country and cottage dictionary. Instead, it is terms like faded, evolved, distressed and eclectic that combine to create this unique style. Pretty wallcoverings and cleverly coordinated soft furnishings are the essence of this style of scheme, with fresh or faded florals and plaids and checks often making an appearance. Country and cottage style is also about using plenty of natural materials, such as wood – old chests and floorboards – and wrought iron bedsteads and curtain poles.

There is something very familiar and unpretentious about the country style of decoration. The scale is always small and under-stated. It also evokes a feeling of traditional values, reminiscent of a time past when even the simplest soft furnishings were hand-made with painstaking detail and pride, creating more of a family heirloom than a simple curtain or bedcover. These days, such items are readily available in the shops and although they may not have had the same love and attention bestowed upon them, they still have a timeless quality.

FABRIC COMBINATIONS

▼ Traditional elements such as antique pine, lace and quilting are the starting points for a cottage look. Add hand-stencilled accessories and floral displays to complete the effect.

UNLIKELY PAIRINGS

▲ This traditional cottage bedroom successfully teams an Adams' style wallcovering with a cottage floral fabric. This may not be the most obvious of combinations, but you can see that it works very well in this setting.

CHECKS AND FLORALS

◀ This is a good example of contemporary country style. Modern printed fabrics in checks and florals team up and provide a fresh contrast against the white painted walls and ceiling.

Meadow freshness
with cornflower blue

A country styled room need not appear dusty and drab or frilly and twee, modern colours and techniques can be employed to provide a successful rustic setting. The secret is to use items that would originally have been found in the pure form of that style of room, but use them in new, vibrant colours or designs, adding a twist to a traditional decorative style.

DISTRESSING FURNITURE

▼ A modern piece of furniture can work well in a country setting if it is softened with a matt paint or a distressed paint effect.

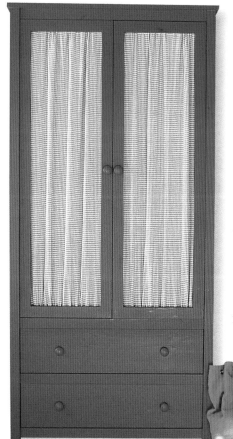

Here, whitewashed walls and wooden floorboards are the basic backdrop for the soft furnishings and furniture. As you would expect, the bed is traditional wrought iron but in a modern scroll design. In place of lace and patchwork, a contemporary quilt and cover dresses the bed in a crisp, traditional yellow and blue deckchair stripe, and as an effective replacement to fussy bed drapes, a simple length of blue sheer fabric is hung over the back of the bed. There is a coolness that accompanies a blue fabric, giving any room a calm atmosphere. But the yellow contrast adds a little welcome warmth to this particular room. Yellow is also evident in the floral fabric used to dress the simple window.

As with any room using almost equal amounts of two colours, plus a non-colour such as white, there is the need for a little something extra to act as an accent to give the colour scheme more of a lift. Here, it is supplied by the curtain fabric which contains greens and reds in addition to the shades of blue and yellow.

A simple tabbed heading has also been chosen for the curtains, which slightly brush the floor, softening the hard lines where the wall meets the floor. These have been hung from a wrought iron curtain pole, once again a modern trend but nevertheless with its origins in the past.

As with all well-decorated rooms, the accessories here are chosen to enhance the style of decoration. Fresh flowers grace the window-ledge and side table, and a simply painted chair offers a seat for looking onto the garden.

FINE FINIALS

◀ Many styles of wrought iron curtain pole are available, varying from the simple shepherd's crook to the more ornate split and twisted finial.

BRIGHT AND SUMMERY

▼ Floral fabrics work particularly well when teamed with checks or stripes.

Simple effects create a
country retreat

**DISGUISING
FURNITURE**

▼ If you are decorating
on a budget and want to
disguise a feature that
is not in keeping, such
as the fitted wardrobe
seen here, consider
painting it a colour that
will blend into the walls.
Avoid adding too much
detailing.

Interior design is no longer as formal as it once was. Purists
would still say, however, that you should only decorate your
home in a style in keeping with the age and genre of the prop-
erty. But when you consider the number of new homes to install
Adam-style fireplaces, coving and picture rails over the last few
years, you can see that this is a view now only shared by a few
designer/decorators. This bedroom, for example, has the proportions and architectural detailing of a typical small family
town house, yet the owner has chosen to give it a distinctive
country feel. The interesting thing is the way she or he has
relied almost totally on paint to create this effect.

The floorboards have been stripped and gently limed. This is achieved with a proprietary liming wax, which is applied to the floor using a dry cloth and then any excess is removed with a second, clean, cloth. Alternatively, apply a coat of white emulsion paint diluted three parts water to one part paint to the floor with a paintbrush. Then leave the floor to dry and finish with a clear matt floor wax. Both methods are very effective, but if you are looking for a heavily limed effect, it is better to use the liming wax and first work against the timber grain with a wire brush.

The walls have been painted in stripes of grey and yellow, yet another simple but very effective paint finish. Before starting to paint, measure and mark out the stripes using low-tack masking tape. To achieve the washed-out look that is on these walls, either use a ready-mixed paint effect glaze in your chosen colours or blend emulsion paint with a clear emulsion glaze following the manufacturer's instructions. Apply the paints to the masked areas of wall using an uneven brush stroke and leaving obvious unpainted areas. Once dry, apply a second coat to build up the soft, cloudy effect.

Finally, the bed has been given a distressed finish on which areas have then been stencilled and decorated using gilding wax. The cost of decoration here is minimal, but with a few country pieces of furniture, the room is very effective.

RUSTIC EXTRAS
◀ There are now a great many rustic accessories available to buy 'new', all of which add nostalgic character to a bedroom.

FINE TEXTURES
▼ A collection of antique and reproduction white linen adds grace to any bedroom, whether it be traditional, country house or cottage.

Antique pine teams with
faded florals for

The colour lemon always adds sunshine and warmth to any room, and here it becomes the perfect backdrop for a blend of country pine furniture and Shaker-style accessories.

Individual, unfitted pieces of furniture give a room a more traditional appearance than fitted furniture of a similar style. But although this room has many of the classic elements found in a country or cottage style dwelling, it also has a distinctively modern feel about it. This can be attributed to the use of plain painted walls in modern colours, the style of lighting, and the simple accessories, chosen to enhance the room.

Details like the soft green peg rail to the right of the bed and the painted fire surround have a simplicity about them which works within the finished room, even though it is true to say that they may not be completely in keeping with a traditional country floral and pine bedroom. This is not to say that it should be condemned as a design mistake. Although there are certain rules of design which must be followed to be a successful decorator, the rules governing contemporary interiors do not stipulate how to mix styles and periods of furniture and furnishings. This means that a very personal and individual range of rooms can be tailored to suit the home.

The mellow tones of antique-coloured pine work very well with the chosen soft furnishings, and the designer has teamed the principal floral fabric with both a small gingham check and a larger check

USING FABRICS

▼ There is a wonderful selection of traditional fabrics available that can be used to enhance a country-style setting.

that cottage look

blanket that incorporates a few of the colours in the main fabric. This pattern combination has also been used successfully in other rooms in this book: large checks complement small-scaled checks which, in turn, contrast successfully with florals. You will also notice the use of a floral rug. It is not true to say that all florals work well together, but because the background of the rug in this room is very open and the design fluid, it teams with the compact floral designs used elsewhere.

GOOD LIGHTING
▲ Side lights not only accessorise a bedroom but can add a variation of lighting accent, creating a different atmosphere at night.

Children's rooms

There is one main difference between a child's bedroom and any other in the house, and that is the child's room should grow with the child. So unless your budget will allow you to redesign the room periodically, keep the decorative scheme flexible, allowing you to change elements to give the room a new design perspective as the child matures.

Most nurseries are decorated to please the parents and not the child. With the exception of supplying a safe, warm environment that offers ample storage for clothing and necessities, the young baby does not necessarily benefit from the decorative borders, pretty papers and frilly curtains that many parents install into their child's first bedroom.

The design challenge begins when you are decorating for the toddler upwards, as their needs change so quickly from being a safe haven in which to play and sleep, to an area in which to study, entertain friends and relax. This, coupled with their liking and disliking of certain types of designs and trends, makes the job of decorating much more complex. To make life as simple as possible, design the room around a limited range of colours and let the accessories change over the years to reflect your child's current likes and dislikes.

TIMELESS DECOR

▼ For a child's room that grows with them, avoid film or TV character bed linen as these can quickly date. Instead, use fresh checks and bright cottons which are easy to launder. For embellishment, stencil a teddy border on the wall or headboard and add teddy buttons to cushions or pillows.

AGELESS STYLING

▼ This style of decoration suits a girl of any age. Avoid bed drapes if you have a busy toddler, however, as she may decide to climb up the drapes which could lead to an accident.

SIMPLY FUN

◀ This furniture offers ample storage and an additional play area which can be removed or turned into a work area as the child grows. There are many styles of cabin bed like this to choose from.

Sailboat theme uses
strong graphics and

A child's bedroom tends to be the area where the designer feels most confident in using decorative elements such as murals and decoupage. Of course, many people will avoid trying this themselves unless they have experience in decorative painting but, as this room shows, some of the simplest painted motifs can have a wonderful effect and need only limited ability and just a little confidence. Here, a sailing motif has been chosen to decorate this fully-fitted bedroom furniture and, to add drama to the scheme, a freehand wave has been painted around the bed and continued into the room at dado height.

ENHANCING SPACE

▼ Blue will always make a room's floor area appear much large, and when used with yellow produces a bright and sunny room.

bright primaries

The bedroom is completely furnished in simple two-tone grey fitted furniture incorporating a captain's bed. This offers extensive storage, and is made from a hard-wearing and easy-to-clean material, a must in a room like this. There is a desk for homework and a pull-out unit at the bedside offering a versatile area at which the occupant can play or put night-time drinks or books. Fitted furniture gives the opportunity of producing a very well-organized bedroom but can look a little hard and clinical at times. Here, though, the furniture design incorporates many different levels. This helps to break up the hard lines, making the layout more relaxed and casual.

It is hard to tell if this decorative scheme was chosen with the furniture in mind or if the furniture was chosen first and then the captain's bed was the inspiration for the nautical scheme. The room could look quite different if the grey surrounds on the furniture were replaced with white or blue on a soft grey base. This would then provide a more integrated colour scheme rather than the contrasting one shown here. Check with furniture manufacturers who can offer a choice of 'trims'.

There are some other, very attractive, decorative details. For example, the border running along the top of the walls has also been used to create a pelmet at the top of the window, and the boat motifs embellish the furniture. These all add interest and, coupled with the red accessories, give life to the scheme.

MOVE IT!
▼ Children's bedrooms will always benefit from movable storage such as these plastic containers on castors. Not only are they useful but the bright colours will also add extra detail to a room.

Cream, peach and
warm brown

An attic bedroom is often full of character and interesting shapes and detailing, but, of course, these details can bring with them their own unique design problems. One of the most common is where, design-wise, in a room with sloping ceilings, should the walls end and the ceiling begin? Should you risk taking one finish over the whole room, or is there a possibility that this will appear to reduce the ceiling height? To prevent that from happening in this room, the timber cladding across the ceiling has been painted in a gloss white, as its reflective quality adds both light and height. Furthermore, the width of the room has been maximized by running the timber cladding right across the ceiling and down the wall to the left. The horizontal lines add visual width to the room.

The basic colour scheme has been designed to be simple and to offer a welcoming warm glow. This is achieved with the use of quite a powerful apricot paint on the walls and with the addition of the mellow timber flooring and furniture. While it is tempting to use light colours in dark, small rooms, if the room lacks natural light, delicate colours and patterns will take on a faded and insipid appearance having very little, if any, impact. This leaves the room fundamentally dull and uninteresting. Instead, such spaces need depth of colour to offer character and brightness, and colours from the

SIMPLE CHANGES

▶ By changing the style of a window dressing, the whole atmosphere of a room is changed. Imagine what the bedroom opposite would look like if the window featured this softly draped blind instead of the more linear blind it currently sports.

for an attic haven

warm side of the colour wheel, such as terracotta, cherry red and primrose yellow, are perfect.

Accessories are kept to a minimum here, ensuring the room looks as uncluttered as possible, but those used have been carefully chosen. For example, the coat peg on the left-hand wall gives storage for bags and coats, and the box beneath the window is in a similar tone to the walls, and does not match the remaining furniture. This ensures the area looks as open as possible, making the window – with its simple blind – the centre of attention in that part of the room.

ADDING INTEREST

▲ Your choice of pictures can add to the colour scheme of a room. Notice how the colours of the subject matter and frames on the two pictures above the bed pick up the furniture tone and the colours in the rug.

Classic nursery styled
on white and

Call me old-fashioned, but I think that traditionally styled nurseries are the best. They evoke traditional values and add a delicate quality to a room, something which cannot be achieved with the use of the brightly coloured fabrics that are growing in popularity. The nursery should be a peaceful place but the difficulty in decorating a room like this is that a child will very soon outgrow its decorative style. So unless you can afford to redecorate in a relatively short length of time, consider how you are going to furnish the room very carefully.

Pastels work best in a traditional setting, and you can either go for the traditional shades of blue for a boy and pink for a girl, or for something a little different such as aquamarine and yellow. Here baby blue and pink have been used to create a soft interior, which has a very calm, serene atmosphere because the blue dominates. A mainly blue goose design wallpaper has been used up to dado height with a white background paper featuring a small pink motif above. This gives the illusion of height in what is quite a low bedroom.

In a room of this size, too much pattern would be overpowering, so the designer has cleverly used plain white for curtaining and soft furnishings. The lace-edged curtains and valance which dress the window, have been gathered with smocking. This can be achieved either by traditional smocking methods or with the use of a commercially bought tape. This detail has been echoed in the tiebacks, and on the cleverly positioned bed drapes. The angle of the ceiling has been used to great effect here with the

powder blue

bed drapes hung directly from tracks attached to the ceiling. This technique can also be used to create half testers, and four posters for full-sized beds in attic or dormer bedrooms. With nurseries, however, be aware of the style of tieback used to secure the drapes as they should be knotted and kept short to avoid the risk of strangulation should they work loose.

SMALL NEEDS
◀ The main items needed for a nursery are a safe place in which the baby can sleep, a chest or small cupboard for storage and a comfortable chair for nursing and night-time feeds. The smallest of rooms will contain all these.

Bed-sitting rooms

As modern properties become more compact and larger traditional ones are divided into flats, there is an increased need to create multifunctional spaces within our homes. Many houses are now designed with dining areas in the kitchen or living room and, for the same reasons, many people find they cannot justify the luxury of a guest bedroom. Instead, they opt for a multipurpose room in which there is a sleeping area. More often than not, these rooms are a sitting room or study.

Before decorating such a room you must decide on its primary function. Is it mainly a bedroom that will occasionally be used to do household paperwork and filing, or a well-used home office offering occasional additional sleeping space when guests stay overnight? The room's main function will dictate the decorative plan and layout of the finished space. For example, filling a room with home office furniture and going to the expense of a concealed bed would be ridiculous if the room were to be used more as a bedroom than a study. In these circumstances, a small desk with an integral filing system would be better placed within the decorative layout of a bedroom. If the idea of a desk in a bedroom does not appeal, a draped floor-length cloth and a small lamp may be all that is needed to disguise this working area within the room.

HOMEWORK

▼ There is a growing trend towards working at home, but unfortunately few of us can afford the space needed to give over a room entirely to a home-office.

& studies

VERSATILE ROOMS

▲ We readily accept the idea of an integral working and study space within the teenage bedroom. So why is it that many people find it hard to consider the idea of an additional sleeping area within the study or sitting room?

DISGUISING FURNITURE

◀ A small desk need not look utility. The painted piece featured here looks perfect in this Mediterranean-style bedroom.

Moroccan-style retreat

SITTING ROOM OR BEDROOM?

▼ This is a great example of a multifunctional bedroom. In fact, it is hard to tell if it has been designed foremost as a sleeping area or a sitting room. The Moroccan theme has such an impact on the room its function seems unimportant; primarily it is a place where you would want to spend plenty of time.

This atmospheric bedroom doubles as a stylish sitting room. Situated at the top of the house, the room has a sloping ceiling and the area under the eaves has cleverly been used to house a low-level bed, which also doubles as an additional seating area. Both ceiling and walls have been colourwashed in a soft blue to add to the height of the space and to soften the angular walls. Many people would say that a plaster pink or terracotta wall would be more in keeping with the Moroccan colour scheme. However, in this case, the room has benefited from a colour that

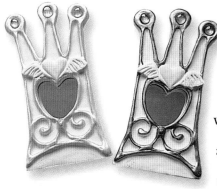

recedes rather than an advancing warm colour which naturally draws in a room. Instead of the walls, the mellow wooden floor and jewel-coloured soft furnishings provide the Mediterranean-style warmth the scheme needs.

As with any themed room, the accessories set the tone, and here are some ideal examples. Moroccan, low-level, hard-wood tables and traditional lanterns add atmosphere but they also help to keep the detailing low within the room. This draws attention away from the relatively low ceilings, making them appear less oppressive.

Hand-painted tiles have been used to create a border around the door frame. Ceramic tiles are used to decorate all rooms within a traditional Moroccan home, so they look perfect here and are proof that they need not only be used in a kitchen.

A Moroccan-style scheme should include a few key elements, such as strong jewel colours reminiscent of the heat of the Mediterranean; fabrics embossed with gold or featuring Arabic motifs; 'magic' carpets to add detailing to the floor, and accessories in ornately carved dark timber and burnished copper. These are all found within this carefully thought-out bed-sitting room. The elements sit together very easily, creating a relaxed room that works equally well for either of its uses.

ACCESSORIZING

◄ It is sometimes difficult to obtain accessories that are exact to the period or style of a room. But quite often an item in a style that is complementary to the room adds personality to the finished scheme. These novel 'crown' mirrors are a good example.

TILING

▼ Moroccan-style tiles can add interest to any room whose decor is based on this theme. There are a number of suppliers, so hunt around for the design you like the most.

Loft room in chic
graphite

HIGH STYLE
◀ Tubular steel and chrome furniture is perfect to complement a room such as the one shown here.

If your home benefits from having high ceilings, as is so often the case in a studio flat or loft, it gives you the opportunity of creating a two-tier layout for your room. By raising elements off the ground, additional floor space is freed up in the room, giving a larger working area. This is the perfect way of adding scope to a room that could be used for more than one purpose.

This room has benefited from a design approach just like this, as the bed has been raised on a sturdy metal structure. Many contemporary interior designers like to use this style of semi-industrial furniture, as it has clean, simple lines and is very functional. In this room, both the bed frame and the simple metal staircase have been finished in a matt metallic paint, which works extremely well within the monochromatic colour scheme.

Many monochrome schemes can appear hard but this room has a softness derived from the mellow tones of the bleached timber flooring. In fact, when you look more closely at the room you can see that it is made up of many tones ranging from the hard black desk, chair and filing cabinet, through to the soft flooring and finally the walls. It is this variation of tone that gives dimension to the room.

Think of the room as it would appear in a black and white

SURFACE FINISH
▼ If you are unable to afford furniture with a modern-style finish such as graphite and steel, try one of the spray paint finishes available in DIY stores.

and steel

photograph; if there was no variation of tone, the room would look flat and uninteresting. As it is, the tonal variety adds dimension and depth to the space.

Each piece of furniture in the room has been chosen for its metallic quality and smooth lines. They each complement the semi-industrial bed structure and continue the contemporary feel of the room. The bed has been dressed using a simple quilt cover in a bright yellow and grey: primary colours are often used to enliven a monochromatic colour scheme such as this one. To further redress the balance, a vase of yellow tulips creates a splash of colour to the right of the room.

SOFTER TONES
▲ Modern styling takes a much gentler approach than that of the 1980s. The grey bed frame and mellow tones of the floorboards are far more comfortable to live with than the starkly contrasting black and white which used to be combined so freely in the contemporary living space.

FOCUS *file*

In the Style File section of this book we looked at specific styles of bedroom and discussed how and why a given room works, while highlighting elements that are important to that particular design of room. So by now you will be very familiar with the options that are available when decorating your home.

I have no doubt that you are also aware that you can create your own unique style of bedroom by combining styles or by using alternative products that are sympathetic to your chosen style of decoration. This section has been designed to give you additional information on the types of product you are likely to use in your scheme. The best tool a designer can have is the knowledge of a large range of decorative products. It is only this that will enable him or her to create countless successful schemes, each unique, and designed to suit an individual room.

Pages 66-69 look in detail at the various styles of canopies and bed drapes that can be created for a room. This section briefly discusses the historical origins of each and gives details on how to achieve the style you desire.

Page 70 sees the beginning of a section on storage. Many people think that designing a room means choosing wall and floor coverings and soft furnishings. Unfortunately, this is not all: a designer also has to ensure that the space available is used to its full potential, and only once that has been determined do colour and style become an issue. Within the bedroom, storage is very important and this section will give you guidance on the types of traditional and modern systems that are available.

Bed linen and soft furnishings are discussed on pages 72-75, once again giving you advice as to what styles work best in what surroundings, together with suggested fabrics for that style of room. There is also an outline on the effects that lighting has on a room, and explains why it is not just a necessity but a powerful design tool.

There is always something we can learn. Enjoy reading this information, and put it to good use in your own home.

CREATING A STYLE

▼ Every room is made up of unique elements. A designer's job is to recognise the important items that set the tone, and to be familiar with similar, alternative products. It is only with this knowledge that you can become versatile and successful.

Bed drapes
and canopies

SHEER DRAPE
▲ This simple bed
drape has been
suspended from little
gilt cherubs. It is very
effective and quick to
create.

The bed is undoubtedly the most important piece of furniture
to be found in the bedroom, and many beds are dressed to be
the focal point of a room. Bed drapes and canopies were histori-
cally not used purely for their aesthetic qualities; four-posters,
for example, were introduced with their heavily draped curtains
designed to be drawn and close out the cold night air. Mosquito
nets, which can be seen in many a contemporary bedroom
scheme, were purely practical. It is only in recent years that we
have recognised the softness and attention they can bring to the
simplest of beds.

The well-dressed bed comes in many forms. For example, the
four-poster is a frame that surrounds the bed with, as the name
suggests, four vertical posts supporting a top frame from which
curtains or drapes can be hung. A half-tester, however, purely
frames the headboard and pillowed area of the bed and it is
either an integral part of the headboard or can be attached to
the wall behind and above the bed. It consists of a back curtain,
a pair of side curtains, and either
a carved wooden or decorative
metal pelmet or fabric valance.
The curtains and fabric valance
are attached to a wooden pelmet
board that is approximately
15 cm (6 in) wider than the bed
and can protrude up to 66 cm
(26 in) from the wall.

**FRINGED
CANOPY**
▶ This bed canopy has
been suspended from
two iron poles attached
via chains from the
ceiling. The fabric is
threaded onto the poles
through two channels
sewn in the fabric.

Coronas are normally semi-circular and are positioned cen-trally above the bed, and the curtains that hang from the corona then draw back to either side of the bed or headboard. They can be made from a simple, semi-circular pelmet board with curtains or a valance attached to the front edge, or can be more ornate, and manufactured from carved timber or metalwork. They are generally prettier and more feminine than the half-tester.

Bed drapes, as the name suggests, are pieces of fabric draped around, above or behind the bed. They can be supported from

FEMININE FOUR-POSTER

▲ This wrought-iron four poster frame has been dressed simply using lengths of white voile. The fabric is attached to the frame with ties, and cream and white roses add decorative details on the inner corners.

CONTEMPO-RARY FOUR POSTER

◄ A traditional four poster frame has been given the contemporary treatment here, with its simple and soft drapes of sheer fabric.

the ceiling or the surrounding walls and their design is limited only by the designer's imagination. From a design perspective, these are the most versatile form of bed dressings as they can be as simple or as ornate as you like. Bed drapes wrapped around a four poster frame and down its vertical posts, for example, can look very contemporary, while a piece of fabric drawn up to create swags suspended from ornate gilt cherubs can add a truly decorative detail to a traditional room.

TROMPE L'OEIL

▶ This paint effect is a practical and artistic alternative to the traditional fabric bed drape or canopy.

CORNER DRAPES

▲ The corner of a room can be the perfect place for this style of bed draping. A pair of curtains and a pinch-pleat valance have been attached to tracks in the ceiling above the bed.

To create your own canopy, suspend a ready-made wrought iron hoop on a chain from the ceiling above the centre of your bed. Then tie lengths of mosquito net onto the hoop. For something a little more ornate, see the canopy featured on page 40.

Finally, don't feel that you need to rely on fabric to dress the area around a bed. The mural is also a clever way to draw attention to the focal point in a bedroom. This form offers endless possibilities from a style and pattern perspective, and has the added bonus of never needing to be taken down and laundered.

Storage *solutions*

BUILT-IN FURNITURE

▲ Glazed or mirrored wardrobe doors can be used to add interest, or can help to break up a long run of matching furniture.

FREE-STANDING FURNITURE

▶ This hand-built fitted cupboard has been combined with additional free-standing furniture to create a traditional setting, with ample storage for both clothes and bed linen.

The perfect solution to storage problems in the bedroom is to have a dressing room, a separate area that is used specifically for the storage of clothes. But few of us can afford to use an additional room just for this purpose, so we need to find other ways around the problem. Clothes are normally the item that require most consideration as the majority of garments are better hung than stored flat, but note the proportion of items within your wardrobe that require hanging space as this will give you a good guide to your requirements. Bear in mind that less frequently

CHANGING LAYOUTS

◄ Ever-changing children's rooms can benefit from free-standing smaller pieces as they can be rearranged at intervals to create a variety of layouts.

used items, such as luggage, bed linen or sports equipment, can be stored elsewhere.

Once a decision has been made on the quantity and form of storage required, then you can consider the decorative style. Think of the finished look you wish to achieve in your bedroom before commiting yourself to the style of storage. Even colours should be looked at in detail. For traditional settings, painted or timber furniture is best, and although fitted furniture offers the best storage solutions, individual, free-standing pieces are the most successful in a cottage or Shaker-style setting. The modern home, however, can benefit from a wider range of styles. Easy-to-clean particle-board and melamine are very practical.

Furniture layout is also very important as it can affect the aesthetic proportions of the room. For example, avoid a run of units at one height down the longest wall of a narrow room as this will draw the eye along the wall, making it look even longer. The best option here is to change the height at intervals or stop the run of furniture and restart it further along the wall.

VERSATILITY

▼ Look out for many of the specially designed features now included in fitted- and free-standing furniture. They include linen baskets and shoe and tie racks.

Bed linen
and soft furnishings

The style in which you choose to decorate your bedroom will have a definite impact on your choice of bedding and soft furnishings. But whatever atmosphere you hope to create in your bedroom, the soft furnishings will play a very important part in creating that finished look.

It is important that the designs and colours chosen are compatible with the colour scheme, but it is also important to ensure that the styles used are practical and functional. Bedding is laundered regularly and should be of a quality and fabric to allow this to happen successfully. Curtains and window drapes,

MAKING A STATEMENT

▼ Many people choose to decorate their room around a favoured set of bedding and curtaining. However, to create a more individual style of room, consider a more decorative style of window treatment such as this one.

STRONG CONTRASTS

▲ The bed need not be the main supply of pattern to the room. Indeed, a plain bed can look striking in a heavily decorated room.

ADDING VARIETY

▶ A blanket or throw adds extra colour and pattern to a room while offering extra warmth to the bed if needed.

on the other hand, should offer privacy and enable you to block out daylight if necessary. This is why many people now choose unobtrusive roller and Roman blinds in addition to a window dressing. The style of curtaining you use need not then necessarily draw backwards and forwards. In fact, I think that a beautifully dressed pair of curtains always look better tied back than when closed at night.

You have a number of choices when it comes to bedding, regardless of the style of room you are creating. Many people find the comfort and convenience offered by quilts and pillow sets are the perfect solution to bedding options and they are

COMBINING FABRICS

▶ Layers of oriental fabrics both behind and on the bed have made it into the focal point in this bedroom.

now available in every style and colour imaginable. Indeed, some bedrooms benefit from the simplicity offered by the styles of these sets, and quilt covers and pillow cases need not lack in detail either. Enclosed openings finished with rustic buttons and simple ties add extra detailing to this practical form of bedding.

Alternatively, you could opt to continue using a quilt and cover but add a decorative throw or quilted bedspread over the top. This means you can use any colour or style of quilt cover under the all-important 'dress' bedcover, which can be full-length or of a size that just conceals the quilt beneath it. If the latter is the case, you will also need to choose a bed valance in a fabric and style to enhance the colour scheme.

There are also choices to be made when selecting a bed valance. You can opt for a simple frilled style or choose a more masculine box pleat or kick pleat. They can also be bound in a contrasting fabric or include details like a row of buttons on the hem edge; even a simple row of over-sized pin tucks can provide the detail required without adding pattern to the valance.

As an alternative to a quilt cover, use blankets and traditional bed sheets to make up the bed. These are enjoying a revival, both because traditional room styles are currently very popular and also because they offer a more substantial feel to the bed when you are in it. The only drawback to this form of dressing is that the blanketed bed takes longer to make in the morning.

CLEAN LINES
▲ In this simple, modern bedroom, a natural silk geometric-design bedspread teams well with the refreshing, sheer, dress curtains.

PATTERN UNITY
◀ This traditional day bed looks very stylish with its collection of check cushions and bedding. Note the position of the uphol-stered screen, giving the room extra privacy.

Lighting

Once the layout and design style of your bedroom have been decided, and before work begins, you need to consider your lighting requirements. There is now a wide range of lighting available. Choices include recessed spot lights, uplighters, downlighters, and lighting troughs, to name a few. And, of course, there are also the more traditional side lights and pendants.

Think of the atmosphere you want to create, both in the day and at night. If your bedroom is multifunctional and you have a work area within the room, your lighting requirements will need to combine the practical with the aesthetic. When working, you

**ACCENT
LIGHTING**
▶ This room has an even light in the day, but look at how the directional recessed spots have been positioned for night-time. This layout will highlight the bed, fireplace and the table displaying the Bonsai tree at the far side of the room.

will need a reasonable quality of light throughout the room, but at bedtime, the lighting should focus on the bed alone, making the work space less obtrusive and a large area would appear more intimate and cosy. Recessed spot lights in the ceiling and side lights positioned at the bedside would be the ideal compromise. Spots give an even light across the room and they can be attached to a dimmer switch to give the option of varying the intensity. Bedside lights offer soft reading light.

Spotlights can also be purchased with a narrow beam, enabling features or accessories to be highlighted. A room in which the bed is an illuminated feature can also benefit from having an additional item or two highlighted, such as a fireplace or a favourite painting. But always consider the balance of the room. Lighting acts as an accent and is very powerful, so it can make a room look one-sided and out of proportion.

EVENING SHADOWS
▲ This is a good example of the effect that simple side lights can have on a room, highlighting the bed and casting shadow on the remaining space.

Stockists and contributors

(UNITED KINGDOM)

Alexander Beauchamp
London Showroom & Sales
Office
2/12 Second Floor
Chelsea Harbour Design
Centre
Chelsea Harbour
London SW10 0XE
Tel: 0171 376 4556
Fax: 0171 376 3435
(Hand printed wallpaper
and fabrics)

Artisan
4a Union Court
20 Union Road
London SW4 6JP
Tel: 0171 498 6974
(Contemporary and classic
curtain rails)

Colefax and Fowler
Tel: 0181 874 6484
(For stockists)

Colorol
Riverside Mills
Crawford Street
Nelson
Lancashire B9 7QT
Tel: 01282 617777
(Fabrics and wallpapers)

Crown Paints
Tel: 01254 704951
(For stockists)

Dorma
PO Box 7
Lees Street
Swinton
Manchester M27 6DB
Tel: 0161 251 4400
(Bed linen and bedroom
accessories)

Dulux Paints
Tel: 01753 550555

Fired Earth
Twyford Mill
Oxford Road
Adderbury
Oxfordshire OX17 3HP
Tel: 01295 812088
Fax: 01295 810832
(Tiles, flooring, fabrics)

Forbes & Lomax Ltd
205b St John's Hill
London SW11 1TH
Tel: 0171 738 0202
(Contemporary light
switches and accessories, as
on page 76)

Gaston y Daniela
UK distribution by
Abbot & Boyd
Tel: 0171 351 9968
(Fabrics)

Grange
Les Meubles de Famille
UK office
PO Box 18
Stamford PE9 2FY
Tel: 01780 54721
Fax: 01780 54718
(Furniture)

Habitat
Head Office
Tel: 0171 255 2545

The Holding Company Ltd
Unit 15, Imperial Studio
3-11 Imperial Road
London SW6 2AG
Tel: 0171 610 9160
Fax: 0171 610 9166
(Mail order with one outlet
in the King's Road,
London)

The Iron Bed Company
Head Office
Southfield Park
Delling Lane
Old Bosham
Chichester
West Sussex PO18 8NN
(Branches in London,
Guildford, Harrogate,
Chichester and Bath)

Jason d'Souza Designs Ltd
London
(Fabrics)

John Wilman Ltd
Culshaw Street
Burnley
Lancashire BB10 4PQ
Tel: 0800 581984
(Fabrics and wallpapers)

Kennard & Company
Long Barn
Clay Hill
Beenham
Reading RG7 5PJ
Tel: 01734 712046
Fax: 01734 712960
Catalogue request line:
Tel: 01734 712047
(Bed linen)

Kingshill Designs Ltd
Head Office
Kitchener Works
Kitchener Road
High Wycombe
Bucks HP11 2SJ
Tel: 01494 463910
Fax: 01494 451555

Laura Ashley
Customer services
PO Box 19
Newtown
Powys SY16 1DZ
Tel: 01686 622116

LeeJofa
19 Chelsea Harbour
Designs Centre
Chelsea Harbour
London SW10
Tel: 0171 351 7760

MFI
For details of your nearest
store phone
Freepages 0500 192 192

Mr Light
279 Kings Road
London SW3 5EW
Tel: 0171 401 2310
(Contemporary lighting)

Pippa & Hale
Head Office
Hollis Road
Grantham
Lincolnshire
NG3 1QH
Tel: 01476 574401
Fax: 01476 590208
(Fabrics)

Pret â Vivrè
39-41 Lonsdale Road
Queens Park
London NW6 6RA
Tel: 0171 328 4500
(Mail order available. Ready
to hang curtains, table
linen, towels and cushion
covers)

The Naked Zebra Ltd
29 Henrietta Street
Covent Garden
London WC2E 7JB
Tel: 0171 240 9124
Fax: 0171 379 5863
(Large selection of African
and South American furni-
ture, ornaments and
accessories)

Shaker
25 Harcourt Street
London W1H 1DT
Tel: 0171 724 7672
Fax: 0171 724 6640
and
322 Kings Road
London SW3 5UH
(Furniture, gifts and
accessories. Mail order
available)

Sharps Bedrooms
Head Office
Albany Park
Camberley
Surrey GU15 2PL
(Freephone 0800 789789)

Spacemaker
Elegant Bedrooms
Head Office
35 Tallon Road
Hutton Industrial Estate
Essex CM13 1TE
Tel: 01277 229223

Specialist Crafts Ltd
PO Box 247
Leicester LE1 9QS
Tel: 0116 251 0405
Fax: 0116 251 5015
(Mail order - large supply of
craft materials)

The Stencil Store Group
Head Office
20/21 Heronsgate Road
Chorleywood
Herts WD3 5BN
Tel: 01923 285577/88
Fax: 01923 285136

Suzanne Malyon Designs
57 Clive Road
London SW19 2JA
Tel/Fax: 0181 540 2634
(Mirror frame designs as on
page 61)

Today Interiors Ltd
Head Office
Hollis Road
Grantham
Lincolnshire
NG13 7QH
Tel: 01476 574401
(Fabrics and wallpapers)

V V Rouleaux
10 Symons Street
Sloane Square
London SW3 2TJ
Tel: 0171 730 3125
(Ribbons, trimmings, tassels
and braids)

AUSTRALIA

Bed Warehouse
57 Magill Road
Stepney
Adelaide 5069

Bed Shed
40 Fourth Road
WA 6112
Tel: 089 497 1411
(Various other outlets in
WA)

Forty Winks
234 Condamine Street
Manly Vale
NSW 2093
Tel: 02 9907 6244
(Various other outlets in
NSW)

Forty Winks
2 Prospect Hill Road
Camberwell
Victoria 3124
Tel: 030 882 7974
(Various other outlets in
Victoria)

Forty Winks
64 Bundall Road
Bundall
Qld 4217
Tel: 074 987 777

Sleep City
HIA Renovata Supa Centa
Cnr Homebush Bay Drive
& Underwood Road
Homebush
NSW 2140
Tel: 029746 9770
(Various outlets in NSW)

NEW ZEALAND

Bed & Linen Centre
345 Great South Road
Takanini
Tel: (09) 298 9098

The Bed Shop Galleria
33 Rumuera Road
Rumuera
Tel: (09) 520 2887

Beds 'R' Us
416 Broadway
Newmarket
Tel (09) 524 5041

The Bedroom Warehouse
176 Trafalgar Street
Onehunga
Tel: (09) 634 11439

European Beds & Linens
6 Marrow Street
Newmarket
Tel: (09) 534 6952

The Linen Cupboard
Level 2
Atrium on Elliott
Auckland
Tel: (09) 379 6633

SOUTH AFRICA

Biggie Best
Head Office
1 Fir Street
Observatory
Cape Town
Tel: (021) 448 1264
Fax (021) 448 7057
(Thirty-nine branches
countrywide)

Boardmans
Head Office and Warehouse
36 Auckland Street
Paarden Eiland
Cape Town
Tel: (021) 510 4700
Fax: (021) 510 3125
(Branches throughout.
Bedding, blinds, lamps,
bedside tables, etc.)

Brass Bedsteads
56 Durban Street
City and Suburban
Johannesburg
Tel: (011) 334 8100

Brass Knight
863 Voortrekker Road
Maitland
Cape Town
Tel: (021) 593 2123
(Brass beds)

Wardkiss Homecare
Blue Route Centre
Tokai
Cape Town
Tel: (012) 72 5000
and
329 Sydney Road
Durban
Tel: (031) 25 1551
and
38 East Bruger Street
Bloemfontin
Tel: (051) 30 1811
(General hardware)

Acknowledgements

The author and publishers would like to thank the following companies and their PR agencies for their kind assistance in the loan of photographs and props used in this book. We have taken care to ensure that we have acknowledged everyone and we apologise if, in error, we have omitted anyone.

For their kind loan of props: Mr Light, halogen lamp, page 12; Gaston y Daniela, fabrics, page 15; The Naked Zebra, hippo, page 16; Alexander Beauchamp, wallpapers, page 18; Albert Smith, Cezanne reproduction, page 20; MFI, headboard, page 20; Sheena Cable, embroidered sheet, page 20; Laura Ashley, cushions, page 36; VV Rouleaux, tassels, page 36; Charlotte Smith, stencilled lamp, page 42 and 49; Jenny King, dried flowers, page 42; Dorma, quilt and bolster, page 42; The Stencil Store, stencils, page 50; Specialist Crafts, special effect spray paints, page 62 and finally Heather Luke for various bedroom furnishings.
For use of transparencies:
Artisan: page 45t; Colorol: page 13b, 30b; Crown Paints: page 29t, 75t; Dorma: page 10, 11tl, 37b; Dulux: pages 7, 8, 13t, 14, 21b, 29b, 32, 50, 54b, 55, 59b and cover; Fired Earth: page 27t, 61b; Forbes & Lomax: page 76t; Grange: page 4-5, 26-27; Habitat: page 44; The Holding Company: page 53, 71t; The Iron Bed Company: title page, 68; John

Wilman Fabrics and Wallpapers: 24b; Laura Ashley: page 43b, 45, 65; MFI: page 49, 52, 70t, 72; Nimbus: page 28t; Shaker: page 15t; Sharps Bedrooms: page 71b; Suzanne Malyon Designs: page 61t.

Picture Credits

Abode: page 11bl, 22-23, 46
Ari Ashley/The Interior Archive: page 69
Elizabeth Whiting Associates: page 11tr and br, 12t, 35, 43, 56, 57, 59t, 63, 66t, 69b
Emily Todhunter/The Interior Archive: page 21t
Henry Wilson/The Interior Archive: page 17, 20t, 38-39
James Mortimer/The Interior Archive: page 75b
Julian Cotton Photo Library: page 47t, 76
Paul Ryan/ International Interiors: page 19
Ray Main/Mainstream Photography: page 9, 16b, 31, 51t and b, 60, 66b, 73t and b, 74 and cover detail
Schulenburg/Jörg Marguard/The Interior Archive: page 40, 42, 58t
Simon Brown/The Interior Archive: page 6
Tim Beddow/The Interior Archive: page 25, 37, 70b

Index